MW01131248

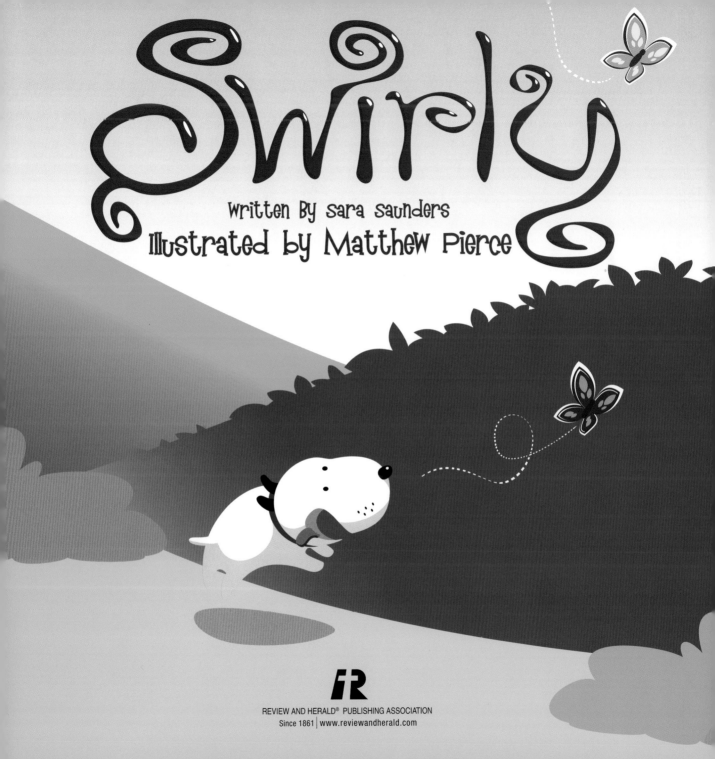

Swirly

written By sara saunders

Illustrated by Matthew Pierce

REVIEW AND HERALD® PUBLISHING ASSOCIATION

Since 1861 | www.reviewandherald.com

Review and Herald® Publishing Association
Copyright © 2012 by Review and Herald® Publishing Association

Published by Review and Herald® Publishing Association, Hagerstown, MD 21741-1119

Review and Herald® titles may be purchased in bulk for educational, business, fund-raising, or sales promotional use. For information, e-mail SpecialMarkets@reviewandherald.com.

The Review and Herald® Publishing Association publishes biblically based materials for spiritual, physical, and mental growth and Christian discipleship.

This book was
Edited by Jeannette R. Johnson
Illustrated by Matthew Pierce
Typeset: Century Schoolbook 13/17

PRINTED IN U.S.A.

16 15 14 13 12   5 4 3 2 1

Library of Congress Cataloging-in-Publication Data
Saunders, Sara.
Swirly / written by Sara Saunders.
p. cm.
Summary: Lila, born in the Blue Country and having lived in the Yellow Country, then the Red, has swirls of all of those colors in her but wonders if she belongs in any one place until a swirly boy's mother tells of Jesus, who was also swirly and has prepared a home for them all.
[1. Multiculturalism–Fiction. 2. Christian life–Fiction.] I. Title.
PZ7.S2576 2012
[E]–dc23
2012024151
ISBN 978-0-8280-2681-9

To order additional copies of *Swirly,* by Sara Saunders, call 1-800-765-6955.
Visit us at www.reviewandherald.com for information on other Review and Herald® products.

Once upon a time a lovely new baby girl was born to a happy blue mother and a happy blue father in a happy blue town in the Blue Country.

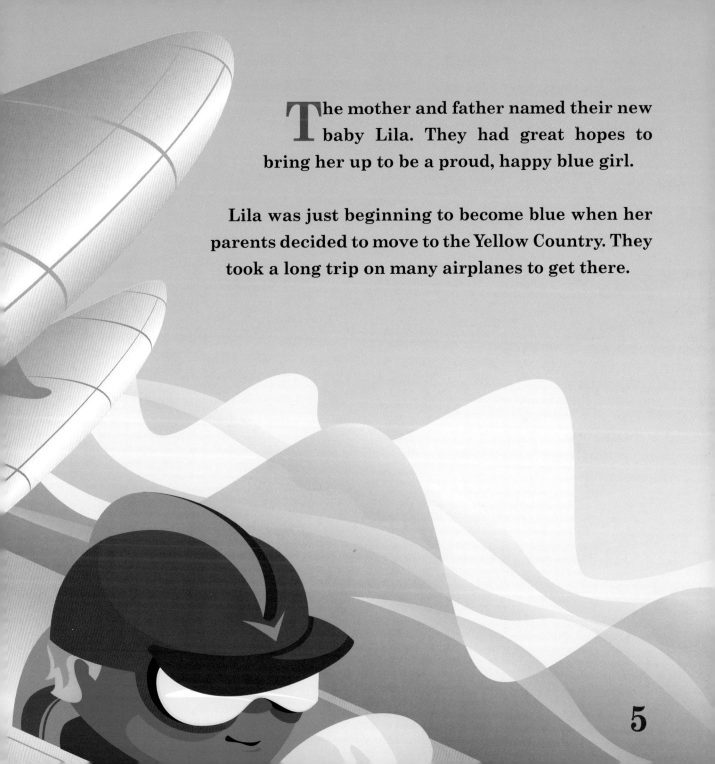

The mother and father named their new baby Lila. They had great hopes to bring her up to be a proud, happy blue girl.

Lila was just beginning to become blue when her parents decided to move to the Yellow Country. They took a long trip on many airplanes to get there.

5

6

They made a new, happy blue home in the midst of a yellow town. They began to learn the ways of their yellow friends and neighbors.

Lila's parents had already grown up to be blue. They learned yellow ways, but they themselves were still very blue.

Lila, however, had not yet grown up to be completely blue. As she grew older in the yellow town, playing with her yellow friends, she began to grow a bit yellow too.

She was a swirl of blue from inside her home and yellow from outside, and sometimes even blends of green.

8

9

10

Lila had lots of fun with her yellow friends, but sometimes she felt different. Her blue thoughts and ways were different from theirs.

"Sometimes, Lila, you just can't understand," they said, "because you're blue. This isn't the place where you really belong."

Lila wondered to herself, *Where do I belong? Maybe this isn't really my home. Maybe I really belong in the Blue Country because I'm blue. But I hardly remember it!*

One day Lila's parents said, "We are going to visit our home, the Blue Country, and see all our happy blue family. Start packing!"

Now I will finally see the place where I belong! Lila thought. She was excited!

14

The Blue Country was exciting and different for Lila! She saw and felt and smelled and tasted many things that were new to her, or that she had only heard stories about before. There was so much blue, just like her. This must be where she belonged!

But Lila was also yellow. As she played and talked with her cousins she noticed they were different from her. They were all blue.

16

Sometimes Lila acted or thought in yellow ways, and her cousins found this strange.

"Sometimes you just don't understand things, Lila. Aren't you supposed to be like us? Aren't you supposed to be blue?"

Lila thought, *I guess this isn't the place I belong either. Where do I belong?*

Lila's parents decided to move to a new place. They said goodbye to their friends in the yellow town and promised to keep in touch.

19

Their next new blue home was in a red town in the Red Country. They began to learn the ways of their new red friends and neighbors.

Lila was still growing up, and as she played with her new red friends she began to grow a little red, too. She was becoming even more swirly!

21

In school Lila made a new friend who wasn't all red.
Deji was swirly like her! He had orange
and green and purple and red.

22

Lila understood a lot of things about Deji, and he understood a lot of things about her. He knew what it was like to want to belong somewhere too! They became very good friends.

One day Lila went to Deji's house after school to do homework and to play. Deji had told her that his mother was swirly too. Lila had never met a swirly grown-up!

While they were doing homework, Deji's mother came to check on them.

26

Mom," said Deji, "We have a question for you." Lila nodded.

"What's that?" asked Deji's mother.

"Did you ever wish you could belong somewhere?" asked Deji.

Deji's mom smiled and said, "I did. But I don't have to wish anymore, because now I know where I belong."

"Really?" asked Lila, "Where is that? And how did you find it?"

"First of all," said Deji's mother, "you should know that Someone very special and powerful is swirly too. Can you guess who?"

Lila and Deji shook their heads.

I'm talking about Jesus!" said Deji's mother. "He left His first country and family in heaven to grow up in a country on our earth. When He was very little, His earthly family moved to another country on earth, and then back to the first one.

29

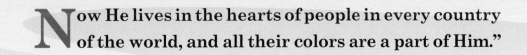

Now He lives in the hearts of people in every country of the world, and all their colors are a part of Him."

Being swirly like Jesus is a special blessing. Being swirly sometimes helps us understand people and ways from all colors of countries better than people who have grown up to be all one color.

SO . . .

If you're red or yellow, blue or green (or maybe every color in between) . . .

Where DO you belong?

Right next to Jesus' heart, that's where!